The Easy Bake Oven Cookbook

100+ Cake, Cookies, Frosting, Miscellaneous, and More Easy Bake Oven Recipes for Girls and Boys

Caroline Jansen

Table of Contents

Note to Parents & Guardians 5

Introduction 6

Bars Recipes 7

Chocolate Peanut Butter Bars 7

Strawberry Bars 8

Apple Bar 9

Granola Bars 10

Oatmeal Fruit Bars 11

Raspberry Bars 12

Cake Recipes 13

Banana Cream Cake 13

Banana Split Cake 14

Birthday Cake 15

Blueberry Shortcake 16

Butterscotch Trifle Cake 17

Carrot Cake 18

Chocolate Cake 19

Cinnamon Coffee Cake 20

French Vanilla Cake 21

Orange Nut Cake 22

Peanut Butter Cake 23

Chocolate Birthday Cake 24

Strawberry Trifle Cake 25

Pink Cake 26

Lemon Cake 27

Oreo Trifle Cake 28

Red Velvet Cake 29

Toffee Trifle Cake 30

Raspberry Orange Cake 31

Berry Cake 32

Mix Recipes 33

Apple Crumble Mug Cake 33

Hot Chocolate Mug Cake 34

Carrot Mug Cake 35

Confetti Mug Cake 36

Peanut Butter Mug Cake 37

Snickerdoodle Mug Cake 38

Pumpkin Mug Cake 39

S'mores Mug Cake 40

Brownie Mug Cake 41

Blueberry Muffin Mug Cake 42

Vanilla Mug Cake 43

Nutella Mug Cake 44

Cookies Recipes 45

Snowball Cookies 45

Sugar Cookies 46

Sugar Spice Cookies 47

Thumbprint Cookies 48

Vanilla Nut Cookies 49

Snow Mounds 50

Chocolate Chip Cookies 51

Santa's Mixers Cookies 52

Raisin Cookies 53

Raisin Chocolate Chip Cookie 54

Potato Chip Cookies 55

Pecan Cookies 56

Miscellaneous Recipes **57**

Jam Pie 57

Cherry Pie 58

Apple Pie 59

Ham Spinach Quiche 60

Easy-Bake Oven Brownies 61

White Chocolate Candy 62

Cherry Danish 63

Cheesy Biscuits 64

Strawberry Danish 65

Scones 66

Olive Poppers 67

Frosting Recipes **68**

Barbie's Sparkling Frosting 68

Peanut Butter Frosting 69

Lemon frosting 70

Crystal Sugar Frosting 71

Cream Cheese Frosting 72

Chocolate Frosting 73

Buttercream Frosting 74

Pecan Frosting 75

Strawberry Frosting 76

Banana Frosting 77

Chocolate Fudge Frosting 78

Blueberry Frosting 79

Delicious Recipes **80**

Cheese Balls 80

Chocolate Balls 81

Bacon Roll-Ups 82

Apple Tortilla 83

Banana Pizza 84

Dessert Pizza 85

Nachos 86

Conclusion **87**

Note to Parents & Guardians

Hi, parents & Guardians! We all know that kids learn best when they get to experiment and play with the things around them. Similar is true for baking! Every kid needs a little freedom to understand baking and its processes on his own. So, let your child follow the recipes from this cookbook in his own way. However, your child's safety is equally important. Though the easy bake oven is simple to use and the recipes shared in this cookbook are also quite easy for kids to follow, but children must not be left in the kitchen or around their easy bake oven alone with any supervision. An easy bake oven is an electrical appliance, so it is also susceptible to electricity incidents. So, parents must take all the precautionary measures to keep their children safe.

- Don't let your kids plug in the easy bake oven without supervision.

- Try to plug in this oven on your own and then prep up the place for children.

- Ensure that all the connections, chords, and wires are insulated and intact.

- Every easy bake oven comes with its own set of rules to use; make sure to teach those rules to your children before they start using the appliance.

- Pick the right tools for your kids! Instead of leaving them with sharp knives, introduce them to mini cookie cutters and other cutters to cut dough into different shapes.

- If you are setting the easy bake oven in the kitchen, then fix a spot that is far from other kitchen items so that you could customize that corner to keep your children safe.

- Check the easy bake oven after every session if it's working ok and make sure to teach your kids to clean once they are done with the baking session.

Introduction

The journey of becoming a great baker and an excellent chef starts from a young age. Kids who are passionate about baking starts to love to bake their treats in their easy bake ovens and share those delights with their friends and family. When children are given complete freedom to play and explore their creativity at a skill they are passionate about, they develop the confidence to follow their hearts and become who they really want to be. Kids who develop a love for baking enjoy baking a variety of cakes and desserts in their easy bake oven. Since cooking in conventional ways using conventional appliances is not appropriate for kids of all ages, so an easy-bake oven provides an easy and fun for kids to bake series of recipes with or without the supervision of their parents.

Our comprehensive collection of eighty easy oven bake recipes is a gift for all the kids who want to bake and cook their favorite treats in their easy bake ovens. Here you will find different sweet bars, recipes, cakes, frostings, cookies, and even Mug Cakes. All recipes are created using easy to find ingredients, and the steps of cooking are so easy that kids can easily grasp the idea of mixing them and then baking them in the easy bake oven.

If you and your kids are looking for some fun and healthy activity to spend some time in the kitchen, then this cookbook is the perfect gift for your children. The recipes in here are categorized according to the cover a range of kid's favorite meals, including sweet bars, cakes, frosting, and cookies, etc. Perhaps, if you are going to surprise your kids with the easy bake oven they have been dreaming about, then this cookbook is the perfect kitchen companion for them. These simple and easy to bake recipes will make learn all the basic about baking and how to get started!

Bars Recipes

Chocolate Peanut Butter Bars

Prep Time: 10 minutes.

Cook Time: 5 minutes.

Serves: 4

Ingredients:

- ¼ cup creamy peanut butter
- ½ cup graham cracker crumbs
- ½ cup melted chocolate

Preparation:

1. Mix crushed graham crackers with peanut butter in a bowl.
2. Spread this prepared mixture in a baking pan and add melted chocolate chips on top.
3. Place the pan in the easy bake oven and bake for 5 minutes.
4. Slice the crust into small bars and allow them to cool.
5. Serve.

Serving Suggestion: Serve these bars with chocolate syrup on top.

Variation Tip: Add whipped cream over the bars before serving.

Nutritional Information Per Serving:

Calories 124 | Fat 9g |Sodium 155mg | Carbs 17g | Fiber 2.3g | Sugar 2.5g | Protein 3.4g

Strawberry Bars

Prep Time: 15 minutes.

Cook Time: 18 minutes.

Serves: 4

Ingredients:

- 3 tablespoons flour
- 1 tablespoon cornflakes, crushed
- 1 tablespoon butter, softened
- 1 teaspoon sugar
- 2 teaspoons strawberry jam

Preparation:

1. Mix butter with sugar, cornflakes, and flour in a bowl.

2. Spread this prepared mixture in a baking pan and leave 2 tablespoons of this mixture in the bowl.

3. Add jam to the pan and spread it over the crust.

4. Sprinkle the remaining crumb mixture on top and bake it for 18 minutes in the easy bake oven.

5. Allow the crust to cool and slice it into bars.

6. Serve.

Serving Suggestion: Serve these bars with maple syrup on top.

Variation Tip: Add whipped cream over the bars before serving.

Nutritional Information Per Serving:

Calories 65 | Fat 2.9g |Sodium 24mg | Carbs 9g | Fiber 0.2g | Sugar 1.1g | Protein 0.7g

Apple Bar

Prep Time: 15 minutes.

Cook Time: 18 minutes.

Serves: 4

Ingredients:

- 3 tablespoons flour
- 1 tablespoon cornflakes, crushed
- 1 tablespoon butter, soften
- 1 teaspoon sugar
- 2 teaspoons apple jelly
- 1/8 teaspoon cinnamon

Preparation:

1. Mix sugar with flour, cornflakes, crushed, butter and cinnamon in a bowl.
2. Spread this prepared mixture in a baking pan and leave 2 tablespoons of this mixture in the bowl.
3. Add apple jelly to the pan and spread it over the crust.
4. Sprinkle the remaining crumb mixture on top and bake it for 18 minutes in the easy bake oven.
5. Allow the crust to cool and slice it into bars.
6. Serve.

Serving Suggestion: Serve these bars with chocolate syrup on top.

Variation Tip: Add whipped cream over the bars before serving.

Nutritional Information Per Serving:

Calories 62 | Fat 2.9g |Sodium 25mg | Carbs 8.2g | Fiber 0.3g | Sugar 2.7g | Protein 0.7g

Granola Bars

Prep Time: 15 minutes.

Cook Time: 10 minutes.

Serves: 4

Ingredients:

- ¼ cup rolled oats
- 3 teaspoons all-purpose flour
- 1/8 teaspoon baking soda
- 1/8 teaspoon vanilla extract
- 2 teaspoons butter, softened
- 1 teaspoon honey
- 1 teaspoon brown sugar, packed
- 1 teaspoon mini chocolate chips
- 1 teaspoon raisins

Preparation:

1. Mix oats, flour, baking soda, vanilla extract, butter, honey, and brown sugar in a bowl.
2. Add chocolate chips and raisins and mix for 30 seconds.
3. Spread this raisins mixture in a greased baking pan.
4. Bake this granola for 10 minutes in the easy bake oven.
5. Slice the granola into bars and allow them to cool for 10 minutes.
6. Serve.

Serving Suggestion: Serve these bars with chocolate syrup on top.

Variation Tip: Add whipped cream over the bars before serving.

Nutritional Information Per Serving:

Calories 54 | Fat 2.3g |Sodium 53mg | Carbs 7.8g | Fiber 0.4g | Sugar 2.7g | Protein 0.9g

Oatmeal Fruit Bars

Prep Time: 15 minutes.

Cook Time: 21 minutes.

Serves: 2

Ingredients:

- 1 tablespoon shortening, soften
- 6 teaspoons brown sugar
- 1 dash salt
- 1/4 cup flour
- 3 tablespoons milk
- 1/8 teaspoon baking soda
- 2 tablespoons rolled oats
- 2 teaspoons apple sauce

Preparation:

1. Beat shortening with salt and sugar in a bowl until creamy.
2. Add milk, oats, baking soda and flour, then mix well until it makes a smooth dough.
3. Spread this dough in a baking pan and press it with your fingers.
4. Add apple sauce on top and bake it for 21 minutes in the easy bake oven.
5. Slice this baked crust into bars and allow them to cool.
6. Serve.

Serving Suggestion: Serve these bars with chocolate syrup on top.

Variation Tip: Add whipped cream over the bars before serving.

Nutritional Information Per Serving:

Calories 180 | Fat 7.4g |Sodium 171mg | Carbs 26g | Fiber 1g | Sugar 10g | Protein 3g

Raspberry Bars

Prep Time: 15 minutes.

Cook Time: 18 minutes.

Serves: 2

Ingredients:

- 3 tablespoons flour
- 1 tablespoon cornflakes, crushed
- 1 tablespoon butter, soft
- 1 teaspoon sugar
- 2 teaspoons raspberry jam

Preparation:

1. Mix flour with cornflakes with butter and sugar in a bowl.
2. Spread this prepared mixture in a baking pan and leave 2 tablespoons of this mixture in the bowl.
3. Add raspberry jam to the pan and spread it over the crust.
4. Sprinkle the remaining crumb mixture on top and bake it for 18 minutes in the easy bake oven.
5. Allow the crust to cool and slice it into bars.
6. Serve.

Serving Suggestion: Serve these bars with maple syrup on top.

Variation Tip: Add whipped cream over the bars before serving.

Nutritional Information Per Serving:

Calories 121 | Fat 5.9g |Sodium 47mg | Carbs 16g | Fiber 0.4g | Sugar 5.1g | Protein 1.4g

Cake Recipes

Banana Cream Cake

Prep Time: 15 minutes.

Cook Time: 15 minutes.

Serves: 4

Ingredients:

- 6 tablespoons flour
- 4 teaspoons sugar
- 1/4 teaspoon baking powder
- 1 dash salt
- 6 teaspoons milk
- 2 teaspoons shortening
- 3 tablespoons banana cream pudding mix

Preparation:

1. Mix flour with salt, sugar, baking powder in a mixing bowl with a hand mixer.
2. Add shortening and milk, then mix well until smooth.
3. Add banana cream pudding mix, then mix well.
4. Grease an easy bake oven pan and spread the batter in the pan.
5. Bake this batter for 15 minutes in the easy bake oven.
6. Serve.

Serving Suggestion: Serve the cake slices with banana cream frosting on top.

Variation Tip: Use crushed graham crackers to add a crust to the cake.

Nutritional Information Per Serving:

Calories 148 | Fat 2.4g |Sodium 283mg | Carbs 31g | Fiber 0.3g | Sugar 19g | Protein 1.5g

Banana Split Cake

Prep Time: 15 minutes.

Cook Time: 20 minutes.

Serves: 8

Ingredients:

- 1 package yellow cake mix
- 5 tablespoons fruit cocktail syrup
- 1 small banana
- 3 teaspoons vanilla ice cream

Preparation:

1. Mix cocktail syrup with cake mix in a mixing bowl with a hand mixer.
2. Grease an easy bake oven pan and spread the batter in the pan.
3. Bake this batter for 20 minutes in the easy bake oven.
4. Leave the cake for 5 minutes to cool on a wire and cut it in half horizontal.
5. Serve the cake with ice cream on top.

Serving Suggestion: Serve the cake slices with banana cream frosting on top.

Variation Tip: Use crushed graham crackers to add a crust to the cake.

Nutritional Information Per Serving:

Calories 355 | Fat 10g |Sodium 452mg | Carbs 63g | Fiber 1.4g | Sugar 37g | Protein 3.9g

Birthday Cake

Prep Time: 15 minutes.

Cook Time: 15 minutes.

Serves: 2

Ingredients:

- 4 teaspoons flour
- 2 teaspoons cocoa powder
- 1 tablespoon sugar
- 1/8 teaspoon baking powder
- 1 dash salt
- 1/8 teaspoon vanilla extract
- 4 teaspoons water
- 2 teaspoons vegetable oil

Preparation:

1. Mix flour with cocoa powder, baking powder, salt, vanilla, and water in a mixing bowl with a hand mixer.
2. Grease an easy bake oven pan and spread the batter in the pan.
3. Bake this batter for 15 minutes in the easy bake oven.
4. Leave the cake for 5 minutes to cool and slice.
5. Serve.

Serving Suggestion: Serve the cake slices with cream frosting on top.

Variation Tip: Use crushed graham crackers to add a crust to the cake.

Nutritional Information Per Serving:

Calories 87 | Fat 4.8g |Sodium 79mg | Carbs 11.2g | Fiber 0.7g | Sugar 6g | Protein 0.9g

Blueberry Shortcake

Prep Time: 15 minutes.

Cook Time: 10 minutes.

Serves: 2

Ingredients:

- 1/4 cup biscuit mix
- 5 teaspoons milk
- ¼ cup blueberries
- 1 tablespoon sugar
- 1/8 teaspoon cinnamon

Preparation:

1. Mix biscuits mix with milk in a mixing bowl with a hand mixer until smooth.

2. Add blueberries and mix until evenly mixed.

3. Divide the batter into two easy baking pans.

4. Grease an easy bake oven pan and spread the batter in the pan.

5. Bake this batter for 10 minutes in the easy bake oven.

6. Leave the cake for 5 minutes to cool and slice.

7. Mix sugar and cinnamon in a small easy-bake bowl and sprinkle the mixture on top.

8. Serve.

Serving Suggestion: Serve the cake slices with cream frosting on top.

Variation Tip: Use crushed graham crackers to add a crust to the cake.

Nutritional Information Per Serving:

Calories 101 | Fat 2.5g |Sodium 188mg | Carbs 18.4g | Fiber 0.8g | Sugar 10g | Protein 1.7g

Butterscotch Trifle Cake

Prep Time: 15 minutes.

Cook Time: 15 minutes.

Serves: 4

Ingredients:

- 6 tablespoons yellow cake mix
- 2 tablespoons milk
- 4 tablespoons butterscotch pudding
- 3 tablespoons cool whip

Preparation:

1. Add 2 tablespoons of milk and cake mix in a mixing bowl with a hand mixer until smooth.
2. Spread the batter in two cake pans.
3. Grease an easy bake oven pan and spread the batter in the pan.
4. Bake this batter for 15 minutes in the easy bake oven.
5. Mix cool whip with butterscotch pudding in a bowl.
6. Spread the cool whip on top of cakes and serve.
7. Serve.

Serving Suggestion: Serve the cake slices with sprinkles on top.

Variation Tip: Use crushed graham crackers to add a crust to the cake.

Nutritional Information Per Serving:

Calories 114 | Fat 4.1g |Sodium 162mg | Carbs 17g | Fiber 2.2g | Sugar 10g | Protein 2.4g

Carrot Cake

Prep Time: 15 minutes.

Cook Time: 9 minutes.

Serves: 4

Ingredients:

- 2 yellow cake mixes
- 1/8 teaspoon ground cinnamon
- 2 pinches ground nutmeg
- 2 pinches ground ginger
- 1 tablespoon carrots, shredded
- 2 teaspoons pineapple, crushed
- 1 teaspoon egg, beaten
- 2 ½ teaspoons water

Preparation:

1. Mix cake mixes, ground cinnamon, nutmeg, ginger, egg, and water in a mixing bowl with a hand mixer until smooth.

2. Add carrots, and pineapple then mix until.

3. Grease two easy bake oven pans and spread the batter in each pan.

4. Bake this batter for 9 minutes in the easy bake oven.

5. Serve.

Serving Suggestion: Serve the cake slices with cream frosting on top.

Variation Tip: Use crushed graham crackers to add a crust to the cake.

Nutritional Information Per Serving:

Calories 93 | Fat 1.9g |Sodium 148mg | Carbs 18g | Fiber 0.1g | Sugar 10g | Protein 1g

Chocolate Cake

Prep Time: 15 minutes.
Cook Time: 15 minutes.
Serves: 2

Ingredients:

- 6 teaspoons flour
- 4 teaspoons Sugar
- 1/4 teaspoon baking powder
- 1 teaspoon unsweetened cocoa
- 3/4 teaspoon shortening
- 1 pinch salt
- 6 teaspoons milk

Preparation:

1. Mix flour with milk, salt, shortening, cocoa and baking powder in a mixing bowl with a hand mixer until smooth.

2. Grease an easy bake oven pan and spread the batter in the pan.

3. Bake this batter for 15 minutes in the easy bake oven.

4. Leave the cake for 5 minutes to cool and slice.

5. Serve.

Serving Suggestion: Serve the cake slices with cream frosting on top.

Variation Tip: Use crushed graham crackers to add a crust to the cake.

Nutritional Information Per Serving:

Calories 83 | Fat 2.1g |Sodium 86mg | Carbs 16g | Fiber 0.5g | Sugar 8.7g | Protein 1.5g

Cinnamon Coffee Cake

Prep Time: 15 minutes.

Cook Time: 15 minutes.

Serves: 2

Ingredients:

- 1/3 cup biscuit baking mix
- 2 ¾ teaspoons white sugar
- 1 teaspoon vegetable oil
- 1/8 egg, beaten
- 1/4 teaspoon cinnamon
- 1 tablespoon milk

Preparation:

1. Mix biscuit baking mix, white sugar, vegetable oil, egg, cinnamon, and milk in a mixing bowl with a hand mixer until smooth.
2. Grease an easy bake oven pan and spread the batter in the pan.
3. Bake this batter for 15 minutes in the easy bake oven.
4. Leave the cake for 5 minutes to cool and slice.
5. Serve.

Serving Suggestion: Serve the cake slices with cream frosting on top.

Variation Tip: Use crushed graham crackers to add a crust to the cake.

Nutritional Information Per Serving:

Calories 76 | Fat 3.5g |Sodium 96mg | Carbs 11g | Fiber 0.3g | Sugar 6g | Protein 1.1g

French Vanilla Cake

Prep Time: 15 minutes.

Cook Time: 15 minutes.

Serves: 4

Ingredients:

- 3 tablespoons vanilla pudding
- 2 tablespoons milk
- 1 package yellow cake mix

Preparation:

1. Mix milk with cake mix and vanilla pudding in a mixing bowl with a hand mixer until smooth.
2. Grease two easy bake oven pans and spread the batter in each pan.
3. Bake this batter for 15 minutes in the easy bake oven.
4. Leave the cake for 5 minutes to cool.
5. Slice and serve.

Serving Suggestion: Serve the cake slices with cream frosting and chocolate shavings on top.

Variation Tip: Use crushed Oreos to add a crust to the cake.

Nutritional Information Per Serving:

Calories 103 | Fat 0.7g |Sodium 297mg | Carbs 24g | Fiber 0.1g | Sugar 16g | Protein 0.6g

Orange Nut Cake

Prep Time: 15 minutes.

Cook Time: 12 minutes.

Serves: 2

Ingredients:

- 1 white cake mix
- 1/2 teaspoon orange zest
- 3 teaspoons water
- ¼ tablespoon pecans, chopped
- ¼ tablespoon coconut

Orange Glaze

- ½ tablespoon orange juice, squeezed
- ½ tablespoon sugar
- 1/4 teaspoon orange zest

Preparation:

1. Mix orange juice, sugar, and orange zest in a mixing bowl and keep this glaze aside.
2. Mix cake mix orange zest, water, and coconut in a bowl until smooth.
3. Add pecans and mix until evenly mixed.
4. Grease an easy bake oven pan and spread the batter in the pan.
5. Bake these cakes for 12 minutes in the easy bake oven.
6. Leave the cake for 5 minutes to cool.
7. Place one cake on a platter and pour half of the prepared orange glaze on top on top.
8. Set the other cake on top and pour the remaining glaze on top.
9. Slice and serve.

Serving Suggestion: Serve the cake slices with cream frosting on top.

Variation Tip: Use crushed graham crackers to add a crust to the cake.

Nutritional Information Per Serving:

Calories 117 | Fat 6.3g |Sodium 80mg | Carbs 72.3g | Fiber 1.1g | Sugar 12g | Protein 1.3g

Peanut Butter Cake

Prep Time: 15 minutes.

Cook Time: 15 minutes.

Serves: 8

Ingredients:

- 1 tablespoon peanut butter
- 2 tablespoons milk
- 1 package yellow cake mix

Preparation:

1. Mix milk with cake mix and peanut butter in a mixing bowl with a hand mixer until smooth.
2. Grease two easy bake oven pans and spread the batter in each pan.
3. Bake this batter for 15 minutes in the easy bake oven.
4. Leave the cake for 5 minutes to cool.
5. Slice and serve.

Serving Suggestion: Serve the cake slices with cream frosting on top.

Variation Tip: Use crushed graham crackers to add a crust to the cake.

Nutritional Information Per Serving:

Calories 297 | Fat 8.7g |Sodium 441mg | Carbs 52g | Fiber 0.8g | Sugar 29g | Protein 3.5g

Chocolate Birthday Cake

Prep Time: 15 minutes.

Cook Time: 15 minutes.

Serves: 2

Ingredients:

- 4 teaspoons all-purpose flour
- 2 teaspoons cocoa
- 1 tablespoon sugar
- 1/8 teaspoon baking powder
- 1 dash salt
- 1/8 teaspoon vanilla extract
- 4 teaspoons water
- 2 teaspoons vegetable oil

Preparation:

1. Mix water with flour and the rest of the ingredients in a mixing bowl with a hand mixer until smooth.
2. Grease an easy bake oven pan and spread the batter in the pan.
3. Bake this batter for 15 minutes in the easy bake oven.
4. Leave the cake for 5 minutes to cool.
5. Slice and serve.

Serving Suggestion: Serve the cake slices with cream frosting on top.

Variation Tip: Use crushed Oreos to add a crust to the cake.

Nutritional Information Per Serving:

Calories 87 | Fat 4.8g |Sodium 79mg | Carbs 11.2g | Fiber 0.7g | Sugar 6.1g | Protein 0.9g

Strawberry Trifle Cake

Prep Time: 15 minutes.

Cook Time: 15 minutes.

Serves: 4

Ingredients:

- 6 tablespoons yellow cake mix
- 2 tablespoons milk
- ¼ cup strawberries
- 1 small cool whip, softened

Preparation:

1. Mix milk with and cake mix in a mixing bowl with a hand mixer until smooth.

2. Grease two easy bake oven pans and spread the batter in each pan.

3. Bake this batter for 15 minutes in the easy bake oven.

4. Leave the cake for 5 minutes to cool.

5. Spread the cool ship on top of the cake and garnish with strawberries.

6. Serve.

Serving Suggestion: Serve the cake slices with cream frosting on top.

Variation Tip: Use crushed graham crackers to add a crust to the cake.

Nutritional Information Per Serving:

Calories 158 | Fat 7.4g |Sodium 148mg | Carbs 22g | Fiber 0.4g | Sugar 14g | Protein 1.5g

Pink Cake

Prep Time: 15 minutes.

Cook Time: 15 minutes.

Serves: 2

Ingredients:

- 2 ½ tablespoons cake flour
- 1 pinch baking powder
- 1 pinch salt
- 1 small drop red food color
- 2 ½ teaspoons white sugar
- 1 drop vanilla extract
- 2 teaspoons vegetable oil
- 4 teaspoons milk

Preparation:

1. Mix cake flour, milk, oil, vanilla, food color, sugar, salt, and baking powder in a mixing bowl with a hand mixer until smooth.
2. Spread the prepared batter in the easy-bake oven pan with a spoon.
3. Bake this batter for 15 minutes in the easy bake oven.
4. Leave the cake for 5 minutes to cool.
5. Slice and serve.

Serving Suggestion: Serve the cake slices with cream frosting on top.

Variation Tip: Use crushed graham crackers to add a crust to the cake.

Nutritional Information Per Serving:

Calories 101 | Fat 4.8g |Sodium 79mg | Carbs 12g | Fiber 0.3g | Sugar 4.3g | Protein 1.3g

Lemon Cake

Prep Time: 15 minutes.

Cook Time: 13 minutes.

Serves: 4

Ingredients:

- ½ cup of sugar
- ¾ cup flour
- ½ teaspoon baking soda
- ¼ teaspoon salt
- ½ teaspoon lemon-flavored drink mix
- 2 tablespoons shortening
- 1/3 cup water

Preparation:

1. Mix sugar, flour, baking soda, salt, shortening, and drink mix in a mixing bowl with a hand mixer until smooth.
2. Spread the prepared batter in the easy-bake oven pan with a spoon.
3. Bake this batter for 13 minutes in the easy bake oven.
4. Leave the cake for 5 minutes to cool.
5. Slice and serve.

Serving Suggestion: Serve the cake slices with cream frosting on top.

Variation Tip: Use crushed graham crackers to add a crust to the cake.

Nutritional Information Per Serving:

Calories 258 | Fat 9g |Sodium 307mg | Carbs 48g | Fiber 0.6g | Sugar 26g | Protein 2.4g

Oreo Trifle Cake

Prep Time: 15 minutes.

Cook Time: 15 minutes.

Serves: 2

Ingredients:

- 3 tablespoons yellow cake mix
- 1 tablespoon milk
- 1 cup small cool whip, softened
- 1 Oreo cookie, crumbled

Preparation:

1. Mix cake mix and 2 tablespoons milk in a mixing bowl with a hand mixer until smooth.
2. Spread the prepared batter in the easy-bake oven pan with a spoon.
3. Bake this batter for 15 minutes in the easy bake oven.
4. Leave the cake for 5 minutes to cool.
5. Spread the cool whip and oreo cookies on top.
6. Serve.

Serving Suggestion: Serve the cake slices with chocolate syrup on top.

Variation Tip: Use crushed Oreos to add a crust to the cake.

Nutritional Information Per Serving:

Calories 298 | Fat 10.4g |Sodium 675mg | Carbs 48g | Fiber 1.3g | Sugar 17.8g | Protein 3.7g

Red Velvet Cake

Prep Time: 15 minutes.

Cook Time: 15 minutes.

Serves: 4

Ingredients:

- 2 ½ tablespoons flour
- 1/8 teaspoon baking powder
- 1 pinch salt
- 2 ½ teaspoons sugar crystals
- 1 drop red food color
- 1/8 teaspoon vanilla
- 2 teaspoons vegetable oil
- 4 teaspoons milk

Preparation:

1. Mix flour, baking powder, salt, sugar, food color, vanilla, milk, and oil in a mixing bowl with a hand mixer until smooth.
2. Spread the prepared batter in the easy-bake oven pan with a spoon.
3. Bake this batter for 15 minutes in the easy bake oven.
4. Leave the cake for 5 minutes to cool.
5. Slice and serve.

Serving Suggestion: Serve the cake slices with cream frosting on top.

Variation Tip: Use crushed graham crackers to add a crust to the cake.

Nutritional Information Per Serving:

Calories 101 | Fat 4.8g |Sodium 79mg | Carbs 12g | Fiber 0.3g | Sugar 4.3g | Protein 1.3g

Toffee Trifle Cake

Prep Time: 15 minutes.

Cook Time: 15 minutes.

Serves: 6

Ingredients:

- 3 tablespoons yellow cake mix
- 1 tablespoons milk
- 1 small cool whip, softened
- 2 Heath candy bars, crushed

Preparation:

1. Mix cake mix with milk, in a mixing bowl with a hand mixer until smooth.
2. Spread the prepared batter in the easy-bake oven pan with a spoon.
3. Bake this batter for 15 minutes in the easy bake oven.
4. Leave the cake for 5 minutes to cool.
5. Spread the cool whip on top of the cake and sprinkle candy on top.
6. Slice and serve.

Serving Suggestion: Serve the cake slices with sprinkles on top.

Variation Tip: Use crushed graham crackers to add a crust to the trifle cake.

Nutritional Information Per Serving:

Calories 271 | Fat 11.3g |Sodium 386mg | Carbs 41g | Fiber 0.3g | Sugar 35g | Protein 2.7g

Raspberry Orange Cake

Prep Time: 10 minutes.

Cook Time: 12 minutes.

Serves: 8

Ingredients:

- 3 almonds, sliced
- 1 package yellow cake mix
- 4 tablespoons orange juice
- ½ teaspoon orange peel, grated
- 4 tablespoons raspberry preserves

Preparation:

1. Mix cake mix with orange juice and orange peel in a mixing bowl with a hand mixer until smooth.
2. Spread the prepared batter in the easy-bake oven pan with a spoon.
3. Bake this batter for 12 minutes in the easy bake oven.
4. Leave the cake for 5 minutes to cool.
5. Spread the raspberry preserves on top of cake.
6. Garnish them with the almond slices.
7. Slice and serve.

Serving Suggestion: Serve the cake slices with cream frosting on top.

Variation Tip: Use crushed graham crackers to add a crust to the cake.

Nutritional Information Per Serving:

Calories 360 | Fat 14g |Sodium 220mg | Carbs 67g | Fiber 0.2g | Sugar 39g | Protein 3.5g

Berry Cake

Prep Time: 10 minutes.
Cook Time: 15 minutes.
Serves: 2

Ingredients:

- 1 packages easy-bake cake mix
- 4 tablespoons milk
- 4 tablespoons blueberries, sliced
- ½ strawberry, sliced
- 2 tablespoons whipping cream

Preparation:

1. Mix cake mix with milk, blueberries and strawberries in a mixing bowl with a hand mixer until it makes a smooth batter.
2. Spread the prepared batter in the easy-bake oven pan with a spoon.
3. Bake this batter for 15 minutes in the easy bake oven.
4. Leave the cake for 5 minutes to cool.
5. Garnish with whipping cream.
6. Slice and serve.

Serving Suggestion: Serve the cake slices with cream frosting on top.

Variation Tip: Use crushed graham crackers to add a crust to the cake.

Nutritional Information Per Serving:

Calories 94 | Fat 3.2g |Sodium 88mg | Carbs 16g | Fiber 0.5g | Sugar 3.4g | Protein 0.9g

Mix Recipes

Apple Crumble Mug Cake

Prep Time: 15 minutes.

Cook Time: 10 minutes.

Serves: 2

Ingredients:

Crumble

- 1/8 cup margarine, melted
- 1/4 cup quick oats
- 1 tablespoon brown sugar
- ½ tablespoon vanilla essence

Filling

- 1 apple, diced
- 1/8 cup graham crumbs
- 1/8 cup walnuts
- ½ tablespoon cinnamon

- ½ tablespoon flour
- 1 tablespoon brown sugar
- 1 drop lemon juice

Preparation:

1. Mix apples with graham crumbs, walnuts, cinnamon, flour, brown sugar, and lemon juice in a bowl.

2. Add this apple mixture to easy bake oven muffin tray.

3. Mix the crumble ingredients in a suitable bowl and divide on top of the filling.

4. Bake the cakes for 10 minutes in the easy bake oven.

5. Leave the cake for 5 minutes to cool.

6. Serve.

Serving Suggestion: Serve the Mug Cake with cream frosting on top.

Variation Tip: Use crushed graham crackers to make the crust.

Nutritional Information Per Serving:

Calories 319 | Fat 18g |Sodium 189mg | Carbs 32g | Fiber 0.3g | Sugar 0.1g | Protein 8.2g

Hot Chocolate Mug Cake

Prep Time: 10 minutes.

Cook Time: 12 minutes.

Serves: 1

Ingredients:

- 2 tablespoons flour all-purpose
- 2 teaspoons cocoa powder
- 2 tablespoons sugar
- 1/8 teaspoon baking soda
- 1/16 teaspoon salt
- 1 teaspoon oil
- 1/2 teaspoons vinegar white
- 1/8 teaspoon vanilla extract
- 2 tablespoons water
- 1 tablespoon mini marshmallows
- 1 tablespoon whipped cream

Preparation:

1. Mix flour, cocoa powder, sugar, baking soda, salt, oil, vinegar, vanilla extract, and water in a mixing bowl with a hand mixer until smooth.
2. Pour this mixture into easy bake oven muffin cups.
3. Bake the batter in the cups for 12 minutes in the easy bake oven
4. Garnish the Mug Cake with whipped cream and marshmallows.
5. Serve.

Serving Suggestion: Serve the Mug Cake with peanut butter frosting and chocolate syrup on top.

Variation Tip: Add chopped nuts to the batter.

Nutritional Information Per Serving:

Calories 100 | Fat 5g |Sodium 305mg | Carbs 23g | Fiber 0.9g | Sugar 14g | Protein 2g

Carrot Mug Cake

Prep Time: 10 minutes.

Cook Time: 12 minutes.

Serves: 4

Ingredients:

- 3 tablespoons wheat flour
- 2 tablespoons powdered sugar
- ⅛ teaspoons ground cinnamon
- ⅛ teaspoons baking powder
- 1/16 teaspoons salt
- ¼ teaspoons unsalted butter, melted
- 1 tablespoon Greek yogurt
- 1 ½ tablespoons milk
- ¼ teaspoons vanilla extract
- 2 tablespoons carrot, grated

Preparation:

1. Mix flour, stevia, cinnamon, baking powder, salt, butter, milk, yogurt, and vanilla, in a mixing bowl with a hand mixer until smooth.
2. Add carrot and transfer this mixture into greased easy bake oven muffin cups.
3. Bake the batter in the cup for 10-12 minutes in the easy bake oven
4. Serve.

Serving Suggestion: Serve the Mug Cake with cream frosting on top.

Variation Tip: Add chopped pineapple to the batter.

Nutritional Information Per Serving:

Calories 340 | Fat 7.9g |Sodium 581mg | Carbs 31.8g | Fiber 2.6g | Sugar 17g | Protein 7.2g

Confetti Mug Cake

Prep Time: 10 minutes.

Cook Time: 10 minutes.

Serves: 1

Ingredients:

- 4 tablespoons all-purpose flour
- 1/4 teaspoons baking powder
- 2 teaspoons granulated white sugar
- 3 tablespoons milk
- 1/2 tablespoons vegetable oil
- 1/8 teaspoon vanilla extract
- 1 1/2 teaspoons sprinkle

Preparation:

1. Mix flour, baking powder, white sugar, milk, vegetable oil, and vanilla extract in a mixing bowl with a hand mixer until smooth.
2. Pour this mixture into easy-bake oven muffin cups.
3. Bake the batter in the cups for 10 minutes in the easy bake oven
4. Garnish the Mug Cake with sprinkles.
5. Serve.

Serving Suggestion: Serve the Mug Cake with chocolate syrup on top.

Variation Tip: Add chopped nuts to the batter.

Nutritional Information Per Serving:

Calories 219 | Fat 13g |Sodium 432mg | Carbs 29.1g | Fiber 3g | Sugar 17g | Protein 3g

Peanut Butter Mug Cake

Prep Time: 10 minutes.

Cook Time: 10 minutes.

Serves: 2

Ingredients:

- 2 tablespoons brown rice flour
- 1/2 teaspoons baking powder
- 1 egg
- 1 ½ tablespoons coconut oil, melted
- 2 tablespoons almond milk
- 1 teaspoon vanilla
- 2 tablespoons peanut butter
- 2 tablespoons honey, melted
- Chocolate chips, as required

Preparation:

1. Mix rice flour with baking powder, egg, coconut oil, almond milk, vanilla, honey, and peanut butter in a mixing bowl with a hand mixer until smooth.
2. Pour this mixture into easy bake oven muffin cups, then add chocolate chips.
3. Bake the batter in the cups for 10 minutes in the easy bake oven
4. Serve.

Serving Suggestion: Serve the Mug Cake with peanut butter frosting on top.

Variation Tip: Add chopped peanuts to the batter.

Nutritional Information Per Serving:

Calories 380 | Fat 20g |Sodium 686mg | Carbs 43g | Fiber 1g | Sugar 12g | Protein 2g

Snickerdoodle Mug Cake

Prep Time: 10 minutes.

Cook Time: 10 minutes.

Serves: 1

Ingredients:

- ¼ cup 2 tablespoons all-purpose flour
- 2 tablespoons sugar
- ¼ teaspoon baking powder
- ¼ teaspoon cinnamon
- ¼ cup milk
- 2 tablespoons salted butter, melted
- 1/2 teaspoon vanilla extract

Topping:

- 1 tablespoon sugar
- 1/4 teaspoon cinnamon

Preparation:

1. Mix flour with sugar, baking powder, cinnamon, milk, salted butter, and vanilla extract in a mixing bowl with a hand mixer until smooth.
2. Pour this mixture into easy bake oven muffin cups.
3. Bake the batter in the cup for 10 minutes in the easy bake oven
4. Garnish with cinnamon and sugar.
5. Serve.

Serving Suggestion: Serve the Mug Cake with cream frosting on top.

Variation Tip: Add chopped nuts to the batter.

Nutritional Information Per Serving:

Calories 361 | Fat 16g |Sodium 515mg | Carbs 39.3g | Fiber 0.1g | Sugar 18.2g | Protein 3.3g

Pumpkin Mug Cake

Prep Time: 10 minutes.

Cook Time: 10 minutes.

Serves: 1

Ingredients:

- 1 teaspoon unsalted butter
- 2 tablespoons gingersnap crumbs
- 1/3 cup pumpkin purée
- 1 large egg
- 1 tablespoon milk
- 2 tablespoons brown sugar
- 1 teaspoon pumpkin pie spice

Preparation:

1. Mix butter, gingersnaps, pumpkin puree, egg, milk, sugar, and pumpkin pie spice in a mixing bowl with a hand mixer until smooth.

2. Pour this mixture into easy bake oven muffin cups.

3. Bake the batter in the cup for 10 minutes in the easy bake oven

4. Serve.

Serving Suggestion: Serve the Mug Cake with cream frosting on top.

Variation Tip: Add chopped nuts to the batter.

Nutritional Information Per Serving:

Calories 305 | Fat 22.7g |Sodium 227mg | Carbs 26.1g | Fiber 1.4g | Sugar 10.9g | Protein 5.2g

S'mores Mug Cake

Prep Time: 10 minutes.

Cook Time: 10 minutes.

Serves: 2

Ingredients:

- 2 tablespoons butter, melted
- ¼ cup graham cracker crumbs
- 2 tablespoons brown sugar
- ½ tablespoon granulated sugar
- ¼ cup milk
- ¼ cup 1 tablespoon all-purpose flour
- ¼ teaspoons baking powder
- 1 dash ground cinnamon
- 1 tablespoon mallow bits
- 2 small Hershey's bars broke into pieces
- 1 small Hershey bar, for garnish
- 10 mini marshmallows, for garnish

Preparation:

1. Mix crumbs with brown sugar, sugar, milk, flour, baking powder, and cinnamon in a mixing bowl with a hand mixer until smooth.
2. Add mallow bits and Hershey's pieces and mix gently.
3. Pour this mixture into easy bake oven muffin cups.
4. Bake the batter in the cup for 10 minutes in the easy bake oven
5. Garnish the Mug Cake with chocolate and marshmallows.
6. Serve.

Serving Suggestion: Serve the Mug Cake with chocolate syrup on top.

Variation Tip: Add chopped nuts to the batter.

Nutritional Information Per Serving:

Calories 345 | Fat 16g |Sodium 272mg | Carbs 41g | Fiber 0.2g | Sugar 12.1g | Protein 2.5g

Brownie Mug Cake

Prep Time: 5 minutes.

Cook Time: 10 minutes.

Serves: 1

Ingredients:

- ¼ cup semisweet chocolate chips
- 2 tablespoons unsalted butter
- 1 tablespoon granulated white sugar
- 1 tablespoon all-purpose flour
- 1 ½ tablespoon mixed egg

Preparation:

1. Add both the butter and chocolate chips to a small bowl.
2. Place the bowl in the microwave and heat for 50 seconds until melted.
3. Mix well, and add flour and egg, then mix well until smooth.
4. Pour this mixture into easy bake oven muffin cups.
5. Bake this batter for 10 minutes in the easy bake oven.
6. Leave the cake for 5 minutes to cool and serve.

Serving Suggestion: Serve the Mug Cake with cream frosting on top.

Variation Tip: Add chopped nuts to the batter.

Nutritional Information Per Serving:

Calories 395 | Fat 9.5g |Sodium 655mg | Carbs 33.4g | Fiber 0.4g | Sugar 15.4g | Protein 8.3g

Blueberry Muffin Mug Cake

Prep Time: 10 minutes.

Cook Time: 10 minutes.

Serves: 1

Ingredients:

- ¼ cup 2 tablespoons all-purpose flour
- 2 tablespoons sugar
- ¼ teaspoon baking powder
- ¼ cup milk
- 2 tablespoons salted butter, melted
- 1/2 teaspoon vanilla extract
- 1/4 cup fresh blueberries
- Coarse sparkling sugar

Preparation:

1. Blend flour with sugar, baking powder, milk, butter, and vanilla in a bowl until smooth.
2. Add blueberries, then mix gently.
3. Transfer this batter into easy bake oven muffin cups.
4. Bake this batter for 10 minutes in the easy bake oven.
5. Serve.

Serving Suggestion: Serve the Mug Cake with cream frosting on top.

Variation Tip: Add chopped nuts to the batter.

Nutritional Information Per Serving:

Calories 301 | Fat 5g |Sodium 340mg | Carbs 34.7g | Fiber 1.2g | Sugar 21.3g | Protein 5.3g

Vanilla Mug Cake

Prep Time: 10 minutes.

Cook Time: 2 minutes.

Serves: 2

Ingredients:

- 1 tablespoon unsalted butter, melted
- 1 tablespoon granulated sugar
- 1 tablespoon egg white
- 1 teaspoon vanilla extract
- 2 tablespoons self-rising flour
- 1 tablespoon whole milk

Preparation:

1. Mix butter with sugar, egg white, vanilla extract, flour, and milk in a mixing bowl with a hand mixer until smooth.
2. Pour this mixture into easy bake oven muffin cups.
3. Bake the batter in the cup for 10 minutes in the easy bake oven
4. Serve.

Serving Suggestion: Serve the Mug Cake with cream frosting on top.

Variation Tip: Add chopped nuts to the batter.

Nutritional Information Per Serving:

Calories 148 | Fat 23g |Sodium 350mg | Carbs 28g | Fiber 6.3g | Sugar 13g | Protein 0.3g

Nutella Mug Cake

Prep Time: 10 minutes.

Cook Time: 10 minutes.

Serves: 1

Ingredients:

- 2 tablespoons all-purpose flour
- 1 ½ tablespoon cocoa powder
- ¼ teaspoons baking powder
- 1 pinch salt
- 1 egg large
- 1 tablespoon granulated sugar
- 2 tablespoons Nutella

Preparation:

1. Mix flour, cocoa powder, baking powder, Nutella, salt, egg, and sugar in a mixing bowl with a hand mixer until smooth.
2. Pour this mixture into easy bake oven muffin cups.
3. Bake the batter in the cup for 10 minutes in the easy bake oven
4. Serve.

Serving Suggestion: Serve the Mug Cake with cream frosting on top.

Variation Tip: Add chopped nuts to the batter.

Nutritional Information Per Serving:

Calories 582 | Fat 27g |Sodium 96mg | Carbs 75g | Fiber 7g | Sugar 52g | Protein 13g

Cookies Recipes

Snowball Cookies

Prep Time: 15 minutes.

Cook Time: 15 minutes.

Serves: 12

Ingredients:

- 6 teaspoons butter, soft
- 3 teaspoons confectioners' sugar
- 1/8 teaspoon vanilla
- 1/4 cup flour
- 1 dash salt
- 2 tablespoons walnuts, chopped
- Confectioners' sugar, for rolling

Preparation:

1. Beat butter with sugar in a mixing bowl with a hand mixer until smooth.
2. Add vanilla, flour, salt and walnuts, then mix well.
3. Make 1-inch round balls out of this dough and roll the ball in the confectioner's sugar.
4. Place 3 balls in the easy bake oven pan and press them into flat cookies with a fork.
5. Bake these cookies for 5 minutes in the easy bake oven.
6. Transfer these cookies to a plate and cook the remaining cookie balls in the same manner.
7. Serve.

Serving Suggestion: Serve the cookies with hot chocolate or a warm glass of milk.

Variation Tip: Add chopped pecans to the dough.

Nutritional Information Per Serving:

Calories 137 | Fat 20g |Sodium 719mg | Carbs 25.1g | Fiber 0.9g | Sugar 14g | Protein 7.8g

Sugar Cookies

Prep Time: 15 minutes.

Cook Time: 5 minutes.

Serves: 6

Ingredients:

- 7 teaspoons shortening
- 7 teaspoons sugar
- 1 pinch salt
- ¼ cup flour
- 1/8 teaspoon baking powder
- 1/8 teaspoon vanilla extract

Preparation:

1. Mix shortening with vanilla, salt, sugar, flour, and baking powder in a mixing bowl until it makes dough.
2. Roll this dough on the working surface and cut cookies
3. Bake these cookies for 5 minutes in the easy bake oven.
4. Transfer these cookies to a plate and cook the remaining cookie in the same manner.
5. Serve.

Serving Suggestion: Serve the cookies with hot chocolate or a warm glass of milk.

Variation Tip: Add cocoa powder to the dough to get chocolate cookies instead.

Nutritional Information Per Serving:

Calories 248 | Fat 13g |Sodium 353mg | Carbs 31g | Fiber 0.4g | Sugar 19g | Protein 9g

Sugar Spice Cookies

Prep Time: 15 minutes.

Cook Time: 20 minutes.

Serves: 8

Ingredients:

- 1 1/2 cups all-purpose flour
- 1/2 teaspoon baking powder
- 1/4 teaspoon ground nutmeg
- 1/4 teaspoon ground cinnamon
- 1/2 cup butter, softened
- 1/4 cup sugar
- 1/4 cup brown sugar
- 1/4 teaspoon vanilla extract
- 1/4 teaspoon lemon extract
- 1/2 cup nuts, chopped

Preparation:

1. Mix flour with cinnamon, nutmeg, and baking powder in a bowl.
2. Beat butter with sugars in a mixing bowl with a hand mixer until fluffy.
3. Add lemon extract and vanilla, then mix well.
4. Add the flour-cinnamon mixture, then mix until smooth.
8. Add nuts and mix well.
9. Make 1-inch round balls out of this dough.
10. Place 3 balls in the easy bake oven pan and press them into flat cookies with a fork.
11. Bake these cookies for 20 minutes in the easy bake oven.
12. Transfer these cookies to a plate and cook the remaining cookie balls in the same manner.
5. Serve.

Serving Suggestion: Serve the cookies with hot chocolate or a warm glass of milk.

Variation Tip: Add cocoa powder to the dough to get chocolate cookies instead.

Nutritional Information Per Serving:

Calories 357 | Fat 19g |Sodium 557mg | Carbs 19g | Fiber 1.8g | Sugar 12g | Protein 2.5g

Thumbprint Cookies

Prep Time: 15 minutes.

Cook Time: 12 minutes.

Serves: 12

Ingredients:

- 1 tablespoon powdered sugar
- 2 tablespoons margarine
- 1/4 teaspoon vanilla extract
- 1/2 teaspoon water
- 1/4 cup flour
- ½ cup jam jelly

Preparation:

1. Mix sugar, margarine, vanilla, water, and flour in a mixing bowl until it makes dough.
2. Make 1-inch round balls out of this dough and place these balls on the working surface.
3. Press the balls into cookies and bake a depression at the center of each cookie.
4. Place 2-3 cookies in a easy bake oven pan.
5. Bake these cookies for 12 minutes in the easy bake oven.
6. Transfer these cookies to a plate and cook the remaining cookies in the same manner.
7. Divide the jelly at the center of each cookie.
8. Serve.

Serving Suggestion: Serve the cookies with hot chocolate or a warm glass of milk.

Variation Tip: Coat the cookies with coconut flakes.

Nutritional Information Per Serving:

Calories 102 | Fat 16g |Sodium 466mg | Carbs 39g | Fiber 0.9g | Sugar 16g | Protein 4g

Vanilla Nut Cookies

Prep Time: 15 minutes.

Cook Time: 20 minutes.

Serves: 8

Ingredients:

- ¼ cup butter
- ½ cup of sugar
- ½ teaspoon vanilla
- ¾ cup flour sifted
- 1/8 teaspoon salt
- 1/8 teaspoon baking powder
- ¼ cup nuts, chopped
- Powdered sugar, to garnish

Preparation:

1. Beat butter with sugar in a mixing bowl with a hand mixer until smooth.
2. Add flour, vanilla, salt, baking powder, then mix until it makes smooth dough.
3. Add nuts and mix well.
4. Make 1-inch round balls out of this dough.
5. Place 3 balls in the easy bake oven pan and press them into flat cookies with a fork.
6. Bake these cookies for 20 minutes in the easy bake oven.
7. Cook the remaining cookies in the same way.
8. Garnish the cookies with sugar.
9. Serve.

Serving Suggestion: Serve the cookies with hot chocolate or a warm glass of milk.

Variation Tip: Add cocoa powder to the dough to get chocolate cookies instead.

Nutritional Information Per Serving:

Calories 121 | Fat 7.4g |Sodium 356mg | Carbs 22.3g | Fiber 2.4g | Sugar 15g | Protein 7.2g

Snow Mounds

Prep Time: 15 minutes.

Cook Time: 15 minutes.

Serves: 12

Ingredients:

- 6 teaspoons shortening or butter, softened
- 3 teaspoons confectioners' sugar
- 1/8 teaspoon vanilla
- 1/4 cup flour
- 1 dash salt
- 2 tablespoons walnuts, chopped
- Confectioners' sugar, for rolling

Preparation:

1. Beat butter with sugar in a mixing bowl with a hand mixer until smooth.
2. Add vanilla, flour, and salt, then mix well.
3. Make 1-inch round balls out of this dough and roll the ball in the confectioner's sugar.
4. Place 3 balls in the easy bake oven pan and press them into flat cookies with a fork.
5. Bake these cookies for 5 minutes in the easy bake oven.
6. Transfer these cookies to a plate and cook the remaining cookie balls in the same manner.
7. Serve.

Serving Suggestion: Serve the cookies with hot chocolate or a warm glass of milk.

Variation Tip: Replace walnuts with peanut or pecan.

Nutritional Information Per Serving:
Calories 248 | Fat 16g |Sodium 94mg | Carbs 34g | Fiber 0.4g | Sugar 23g | Protein 4.9g

Chocolate Chip Cookies

Prep Time: 15 minutes.

Cook Time: 12 minutes.

Serves: 6

Ingredients:

- 1 tablespoon sugar
- 1 tablespoon packed brown sugar
- 2 teaspoons margarine
- 1/8 teaspoon baking powder
- 1/8 teaspoon vanilla extract
- 1 teaspoon water
- 3 tablespoons all-purpose flour
- 4 teaspoons chocolate chips

Preparation:

1. Mix sugar, sugar, margarine, baking powder, vanilla extract, water, and flour in a mixing bowl with a hand mixer until it makes a smooth dough.

2. Add chocolate chips and mix them evenly.

3. Make 12- (1-inch round) balls out of this dough and roll the ball in the confectioner's sugar.

4. Place 3 balls in the easy bake oven pan and press them into flat cookies with a fork.

5. Bake these cookies for 12 minutes in the easy bake oven.

6. Transfer these cookies to a plate and cook the remaining cookie balls in the same manner.

7. Serve.

Serving Suggestion: Serve the cookies with hot chocolate or a warm glass of milk.

Variation Tip: Add cocoa powder to the dough to get chocolate cookies instead.

Nutritional Information Per Serving:

Calories 178 | Fat 21g |Sodium 146mg | Carbs 28g | Fiber 0.1g | Sugar 14g | Protein 3g

Santa's Mixers Cookies

Prep Time: 15 minutes.

Cook Time: 20 minutes.

Serves: 6

Ingredients:

- ½ cup butter
- ½ cup of sugar
- 1 tablespoon milk
- ½ teaspoon vanilla
- 1 ¼ cups all-purpose flour
- ½ cup red candied cherries, chopped
- ¼ cup pecans, chopped
- ½ cup flaked coconut

Preparation:

1. Beat butter with sugar in a mixing bowl with a hand mixer until fluffy.
2. Add vanilla, milk, and flour then mix well.
3. Add pecans, flaked coconut and cherries and mix evenly.
4. Wrap the dough in a plastic sheet, then refrigerate for 1 hour.
5. Add nuts and mix well.
6. Make 1-inch round balls out of this dough.
7. Place 3 balls in the easy bake oven pan and press them into flat cookies with a fork.
8. Bake these cookies for 20 minutes in the easy bake oven.
9. Cook the remaining cookies in the same way.
10. Serve.

Serving Suggestion: Serve the cookies with hot chocolate or a warm glass of milk.

Variation Tip: Add cocoa powder to the dough to get chocolate cookies instead.

Nutritional Information Per Serving:

Calories 151 | Fat 4g |Sodium 236mg | Carbs 29.1g | Fiber 0.3g | Sugar 10g | Protein 3g

Raisin Cookies

Prep Time: 15 minutes.

Cook Time: 7 minutes.

Serves: 8

Ingredients:

- 3 teaspoons sugar
- 1 1/2 teaspoons shortening
- 6 teaspoons flour
- 1/8 teaspoon baking powder
- 1/8 teaspoon vanilla
- 3 teaspoons milk
- 1 tablespoon raisins

Preparation:

1. Beat butter with sugar in a mixing bowl with a hand mixer until smooth.
2. Add vanilla, flour, salt and walnuts, then mix well.
3. Make 1-inch round balls out of this dough.
4. Place 3 balls in the easy bake oven pan and press them into flat cookies with a fork.
5. Bake these cookies for 7 minutes in the easy bake oven.
6. Transfer these cookies to a plate.
7. Serve.

Serving Suggestion: Serve the cookies with hot chocolate or a warm glass of milk.

Variation Tip: Add cocoa powder to the dough to get chocolate cookies instead.

Nutritional Information Per Serving:

Calories 378 | Fat 7g |Sodium 316mg | Carbs 26.2g | Fiber 0.3g | Sugar 13g | Protein 6g

Raisin Chocolate Chip Cookie

Prep Time: 15 minutes.

Cook Time: 5 minutes.

Serves: 9

Ingredients:

- 1 package children's cookie mix
- 2 teaspoons water
- 1 tablespoon raisins
- 1 tablespoon mini chocolate chips
- Sugar, to roll

Preparation:

1. Mix water with cookie mix in a bowl until it makes smooth dough.
2. Add chocolate chips and raisins, then mix evenly.
3. Make 1-inch round balls out of this dough and roll the ball in the confectioner's sugar.
4. Place 3 balls in the easy bake oven pan and press them into flat cookies with a fork.
5. Bake these cookies for 5 minutes in the easy bake oven.
6. Transfer these cookies to a plate and cook the remaining cookie balls in the same manner.
7. Serve.

Serving Suggestion: Serve the cookies with hot chocolate or a warm glass of milk.

Variation Tip: Add cocoa powder to the dough to get chocolate cookies instead.

Nutritional Information Per Serving:

Calories 115 | Fat 15g |Sodium 634mg | Carbs 24.3g | Fiber 1.4g | Sugar 13g | Protein 3.3g

Potato Chip Cookies

Prep Time: 15 minutes.

Cook Time: 10 minutes.

Serves: 8

Ingredients:

- 2 tablespoons shortening
- 2 tablespoons sugar
- 2 tablespoons brown sugar
- 1/4 egg
- 1/8 teaspoon vanilla extract
- 1/4 cup all-purpose flour
- 1/8 teaspoon baking soda
- 1/8 teaspoon salt
- 1/4 cup potato chips, crushed

Preparation:

1. Beat egg, sugar, brown sugar, shortening in a mixing bowl with a hand mixer until smooth.
2. Add vanilla, flour, salt, baking soda, and crushed potato chips, then mix well.
3. Make 1-inch round balls out of this dough.
4. Place 3 balls in the easy bake oven pan and press them into flat cookies with a fork.
5. Bake these cookies for 10 minutes in the easy bake oven.
6. Transfer these cookies to a plate and cook the remaining cookie balls in the same manner.
7. Serve.

Serving Suggestion: Serve the cookies with hot chocolate or a warm glass of milk.

Variation Tip: Add cocoa powder to the dough to get chocolate cookies instead.

Nutritional Information Per Serving:

Calories 246 | Fat 15g |Sodium 220mg | Carbs 40.3g | Fiber 2.4g | Sugar 12g | Protein 2.4g

Pecan Cookies

Prep Time: 15 minutes.

Cook Time: 20 minutes.

Serves: 6

Ingredients:

- 1 cup all-purpose flour
- 1 pinch ground cinnamon
- 1 pinch Salt
- 8 tablespoons unsalted butter softened
- 1/4 cup sugar
- 1/2 teaspoon vanilla extract
- 1/2 cup toasted pecans, chopped
- Powdered sugar, for dusting

Preparation:

1. Mix flour, cinnamon, salt, butter, sugar, vanilla extract in a mixing bowl with a hand mixer until smooth.
2. Add pecans and wrap the dough in a plastic sheet, then refrigerate for 1 hour.
3. Add nuts and mix well.
4. Make 1-inch round balls out of this dough.
5. Place 3 balls in the easy bake oven pan and press them into flat cookies with a fork.
6. Bake these cookies for 20 minutes in the easy bake oven.
7. Coat the cookies with confectioner's sugar.
8. Serve.

Serving Suggestion: Serve the cookies with hot chocolate or a warm glass of milk.

Variation Tip: Add cocoa powder to the dough to get chocolate cookies instead.

Nutritional Information Per Serving:
Calories 338 | Fat 24g |Sodium 620mg | Carbs 58.3g | Fiber 2.4g | Sugar 19g | Protein 5.4g

Miscellaneous Recipes

Jam Pie

Prep Time: 15 minutes.

Cook Time: 30 minutes.

Serves: 6

Ingredients:

- 1/3 cup pie crust mix
- 4 teaspoons water
- 2 tablespoons jam filling

Preparation:

1. Mix pie crust mix with water in a bowl until smooth.
2. Divide the dough in half and spread one half in the easy bake oven pan.
3. Add filling to this dough crust and spread it evenly.
4. Roll the other half of the dough and place them over the filling.
5. Pinch and press the edges of the pie with your fingers and cut a cross on top of the pie.
6. Bake this pie in the easy bake oven for 30 minutes.
7. Serve.

Serving Suggestion: Serve this pie with a hot beverage.

Variation Tip: Add fruit bits to the filling.

Nutritional Information Per Serving:

Calories 121 | Fat 10.1g |Sodium 380mg | Carbs 25.3g | Fiber 2.4g | Sugar 12g | Protein 2.1g

Cherry Pie

Prep Time: 15 minutes.

Cook Time: 30 minutes.

Serves: 6

Ingredients:

- 1/3 cup pie crust mix
- 4 teaspoons water
- 6 teaspoons cherry pie filling

Preparation:

1. Mix pie crust mix with water in a bowl until smooth.
2. Divide the dough in half and spread one half in the easy bake oven pan.
3. Add the cherry filling to this dough crust and spread it evenly.
4. Roll the other half of the dough and place them over the filling.
5. Pinch and press the edges of the pie with your fingers and cut a cross on top of the pie.
6. Bake this pie in the easy bake oven for 30 minutes.
7. Serve.

Serving Suggestion: Serve this pie with hot chocolate or a warm glass of milk.

Variation Tip: Add chopped cherries to the filling.

Nutritional Information Per Serving:

Calories 178 | Fat 3.8g |Sodium 620mg | Carbs 23.3g | Fiber 2.4g | Sugar 13g | Protein 5.4g

Apple Pie

Prep Time: 15 minutes.

Cook Time: 30 minutes.

Serves: 6

Ingredients:

- 1/3 cup pie crust mix
- 4 teaspoons water
- 6 teaspoons apple pie filling

Preparation:

1. Mix pie crust mix with water in a bowl until smooth.
2. Divide the dough in half and spread one half in the easy bake oven pan.
3. Add apple pie filling to this dough crust and spread it evenly.
4. Roll the other half of the dough and place them over the filling.
5. Pinch and press the edges of the pie with your fingers and cut a cross on top of the pie.
6. Bake this pie in the easy bake oven for 30 minutes.
7. Serve.

Serving Suggestion: Serve this pie with hot chocolate or a warm glass of milk.

Variation Tip: Add chopped nuts to the filling.

Nutritional Information Per Serving:

Calories 304 | Fat 31g |Sodium 834mg | Carbs 31.4g | Fiber 0.2g | Sugar 13g | Protein 4.6g

Ham Spinach Quiche

Prep Time: 15 minutes.

Cook Time: 15 minutes.

Serves: 4

Ingredients:

- 1 1/3 cups all-purpose flour, sifted
- 1/4 teaspoon salt
- 4 tablespoons butter, cubed
- ¼ cup vegetable shortening, cubed
- 4 tablespoons water, ice cold

Filling:

- 2 eggs
- 1/4 cup cream
- 1/8 cup ham, diced
- 1/4 cup cheese, grated
- 1/4 cup spinach, chopped

Preparation:

1. Mix flour with salt, butter, shortening, and water in a pastry blender.
2. Spread this dough in the easy bake oven pan and cover to refrigerate for 30 minutes.
3. Beat eggs with cream in a bowl.
4. Add cheese, ham, and spinach, then mix well.
5. Pour this filling into the quiche crust.
6. Preheat your easy bake oven for 15 minutes.
7. Bake the prepared quiche for 30 minutes in the easy bake oven.
8. Slice and serve.

Serving Suggestion: Serve this quiche with toasted bread slices.

Variation Tip: Add chopped sausage to the filling mixture.

Nutritional Information Per Serving:

Calories 241 | Fat 4g |Sodium 547mg | Carbs 36.4g | Fiber 1.2g | Sugar 1g | Protein 13.3g

Easy-Bake Oven Brownies

Prep Time: 15 minutes.

Cook Time: 12 minutes.

Serves: 4

Ingredients:

- 2 tablespoons sugar
- 2 ½ tablespoons flour
- 1 teaspoon oil
- 1/8 tablespoon baking powder
- 1/8 teaspoon vanilla extract
- 2 teaspoons chocolate syrup
- 2 teaspoons milk
- 1 teaspoon baking cocoa

Preparation:

1. Mix flour with sugar, oil, baking powder, vanilla extract, chocolate syrup, milk, and baking cocoa in a mixing bowl until smooth.
2. Divide this batter in the easy bake oven muffin pan.
3. Bake the brownies for 12 minutes in the easy bake oven.
4. Allow the brownies to cool.
5. Serve.

Serving Suggestion: Serve these brownies with an ice-cream scoop on top.

Variation Tip: Add chopped nuts to the batter before baking.

Nutritional Information Per Serving:

Calories 118 | Fat 5.7g |Sodium 124mg | Carbs 27g | Fiber 0.1g | Sugar 13g | Protein 4.9g

White Chocolate Candy

Prep Time: 15 minutes.

Cook Time: 15 minutes.

Serves: 6

Ingredients:

- 1/4 cup white chocolate chips
- 2 teaspoons butter

Preparation:

1. Add chocolate chips and butter to the easy baking oven pan.
2. Melt this mixture for 15 minutes in the easy bake oven.
3. Mix well and pour this melt into the candy molds.
4. Allow the candies to cool and refrigerate for 30 minutes.
5. Remove the candies from the molds.
6. Serve.

Serving Suggestion: Serve the candies with chocolate syrup on top.

Variation Tip: Add chopped nuts to the melted white chocolate.

Nutritional Information Per Serving:

Calories 191 | Fat 2.2g |Sodium 276mg | Carbs 17.7g | Fiber 0.9g | Sugar 9g | Protein 2.8g

Cherry Danish

Prep Time: 15 minutes.

Cook Time: 15 minutes.

Serves: 4

Ingredients:

- ¼ cup biscuit mix
- ½ tablespoon margarine
- 3/4 teaspoon sugar
- 4 teaspoons milk
- 1/2 tablespoon cherry pie filling

Preparation:

1. Mix biscuit mix with margarine, sugar, and milk in a bowl until smooth.
2. Spread this prepared mixture in the easy bake oven and top the batter with cherry pie filling.
3. Bake these layers for 15 minutes in the easy bake oven.
4. Slice and serve.

Serving Suggestion: Serve the cherry Danish with fresh cherries on top.

Variation Tip: Add crushed biscuit topping for a crispy taste.

Nutritional Information Per Serving:

Calories 224 | Fat 5g |Sodium 432mg | Carbs 33.1g | Fiber 0.3g | Sugar 21g | Protein 5.7g

Cheesy Biscuits

Prep Time: 15 minutes.

Cook Time: 15 minutes.

Serves: 4

Ingredients:

- 1/2 cup baking mix
- 2 tablespoons 2 teaspoons milk
- 2 tablespoons cheddar cheese, shredded
- 1 tablespoon parmesan cheese

Topping:

- 1 tablespoon butter
- 1/8 garlic powder
- ¼ teaspoon dried parsley

Preparation:

1. Mix baking mix with milk, cheddar cheese, and parmesan cheese in a bowl.
2. Drop the batter spoon by spoon into biscuits on to easy bake pan.
3. Bake the prepared biscuits for 15 minutes in the easy bake oven.
4. Mix butter with garlic powder and parsley.
5. Sprinkle this butter mixture over the biscuits.
6. Serve.

Serving Suggestion: Serve these biscuits with cheese dip.

Variation Tip: Add crumbled bacon to the biscuit dough.

Nutritional Information Per Serving:

Calories 305 | Fat 25g |Sodium 532mg | Carbs 23g | Fiber 0.4g | Sugar 12g | Protein 8.3g

Strawberry Danish

Prep Time: 15 minutes.

Cook Time: 15 minutes.

Serves: 4

Ingredients:

- ¼ cup biscuit mix
- 1/2 tablespoon margarine
- ¾ teaspoon sugar
- 4 teaspoons milk
- ½ tablespoon strawberry pie filling

Preparation:

5. Mix biscuit mix with margarine, sugar, and milk in a bowl until smooth.

6. Spread this prepared mixture in the easy bake oven and top the batter with strawberry pie filling.

7. Bake these layers for 15 minutes in the easy bake oven.

8. Slice and serve.

Serving Suggestion: Serve the cherry Danish with fresh strawberries on top.

Variation Tip: Add crushed biscuit topping for a crispy taste.

Nutritional Information Per Serving:

Calories 205 | Fat 15g |Sodium 532mg | Carbs 23g | Fiber 0.4g | Sugar 14g | Protein 1.3g

Scones

Prep Time: 15 minutes.

Cook Time: 15 minutes.

Serves: 6

Ingredients:

- 1 tablespoon sour cream
- 1/8 teaspoon baking soda
- 1/3 cup all-purpose flour
- 1 tablespoon sugar
- 1/8 teaspoon baking powder
- 1/8 teaspoon cream of tartar
- 1/8 teaspoon salt
- 1 tablespoon butter
- 1 tablespoon raisins

Preparation:

1. Mix sour cream, baking soda, flour, sugar, baking powder, cream of tartar, salt, and butter in a mixing bowl until it makes smooth dough.

2. Add raisins, mix evenly, then roll this dough on a floured surface into ½ inch thick round.

3. Slice this sheet into wedges and place them on the baking sheet.

4. Place the scones in the easy bake oven pan.

5. Bake the scones for 15 minutes in the easy bake oven.

6. Serve.

Serving Suggestion: Serve the scones with chocolate syrup on top.

Variation Tip: Add chopped nuts or blueberries to the scones.

Nutritional Information Per Serving:

Calories 115 | Fat 13g |Sodium 232mg | Carbs 27g | Fiber 0.4g | Sugar 16g | Protein 3.3g

Olive Poppers

Prep Time: 15 minutes.

Cook Time: 25 minutes.

Serves: 12

Ingredients:

- 2 tablespoons butter
- 24 olives, hollowed
- 1 ½ cups sharp cheddar cheese, grated
- 9 tablespoons all-purpose flour
- ¾ teaspoon hot pepper sauce
- ½ teaspoon salt
- 2 tablespoons milk

Preparation:

1. Mix melted butter with flour, pepper sauce, milk, and salt in a bowl until smooth.
2. Dip each olive in the flour batter and coat with the cheddar cheese.
3. Place these olives in the easy bake oven pan.
4. Bake the olives poppers for 25 minutes in the easy bake oven.
5. Serve warm.

Serving Suggestion: Serve the poppers with tomato ketchup on the side.

Variation Tip: Rolls the coated olives in breadcrumbs before baking.

Nutritional Information Per Serving:

Calories 135 | Fat 11g |Sodium 122mg | Carbs 35g | Fiber 0.4g | Sugar 2.4g | Protein 13g

Frosting Recipes

Barbie's Sparkling Frosting

Prep Time: 15 minutes.

Cook Time: 0 minutes.

Serves: 6

Ingredients:

- 4 teaspoons vegetable shortening
- 2/3 cup powdered sugar
- 1/4 teaspoon vanilla
- 2 teaspoons milk
- Colored sugar crystals for decoration

Preparation:

1. Beat sugar and shortening in a blender until creamy.
2. Add milk and vanilla and beat well.
3. Garnish with sugar crystals.
4. Serve.

Serving Suggestion: Add the frosting to a piping bag and pipe it on top of plain cakes and muffins.

Variation Tip: Add cream cheese to the frosting to make it richer in taste.

Nutritional Information Per Serving:

Calories 118 | Fat 4.3g |Sodium 532mg | Carbs 20g | Fiber 0.4g | Sugar 20g | Protein 0.1g

Peanut Butter Frosting

Prep Time: 15 minutes.

Cook Time: 0 minutes.

Serves: 6

Ingredients:

- 2 cups icing sugar, sifted
- 3 tablespoons of milk powder
- 6 tablespoons peanut butter

Preparation:

1. Blend milk powder with sugar and peanut butter in a pastry blender.
2. Mix this frosting with ¾ cup water before using.
3. Refrigerate this frosting for 30 minutes.
4. Serve.

Serving Suggestion: Add the frosting to a piping bag and pipe it on top of plain cakes and muffins.

Variation Tip: Add cream cheese to the frosting to make it richer in taste.

Nutritional Information Per Serving:

Calories 105 | Fat 12g |Sodium 532mg | Carbs 13g | Fiber 0.4g | Sugar 9g | Protein 1.3g

Lemon frosting

Prep Time: 15 minutes.

Cook Time: 0 minutes.

Serves: 6

Ingredients:

- 1/4 cup powdered sugar
- 1 teaspoon lemon juice
- 1 teaspoon water

Preparation:

1. Beat sugar with water and lemon juice in a blender until it makes a thick mixture.
2. Refrigerate this frosting for 30 minutes.
3. Serve.

Serving Suggestion: Pour it on top of plain cakes and muffins.

Variation Tip: Add cream to the frosting to make it richer in taste.

Nutritional Information Per Serving:

Calories 98 | Fat 5g |Sodium 122mg | Carbs 21g | Fiber 0.3g | Sugar 12g | Protein 0.3g

Crystal Sugar Frosting

Prep Time: 15 minutes.

Cook Time: 0 minutes.

Serves: 2

Ingredients:

- 4 teaspoons vegetable shortening
- 2/3 cup powdered sugar
- ¼ teaspoon vanilla extract
- 1 teaspoon milk

Preparation:

1. Beat shortening with sugar, vanilla, and milk in a blender until creamy.
2. Refrigerate this frosting for 30 minutes.
3. Serve.

Serving Suggestion: Add the frosting to a piping bag and pipe it on top of plain cakes and muffins.

Variation Tip: Add cream cheese to the frosting to make it richer in taste.

Nutritional Information Per Serving:

Calories 119 | Fat 22g |Sodium 132mg | Carbs 32g | Fiber 1.1g | Sugar 18g | Protein 1.3g

Cream Cheese Frosting

Prep Time: 15 minutes.

Cook Time: 0 minutes.

Serves: 6

Ingredients:

- 1 cup confectioners' sugar
- 4 1/2 teaspoons milk powder
- 3 tablespoons cream cheese

Preparation:

1. Beat cream cheese with sugar and milk powder in a blender until cream.
2. Refrigerate this frosting for 30 minutes.
3. Serve.

Serving Suggestion: Add the frosting to a piping bag and pipe it on top of plain cakes and muffins.

Variation Tip: Add chopped nuts to the frosting to make it richer in taste.

Nutritional Information Per Serving:

Calories 201 | Fat 25g |Sodium 212mg | Carbs 21g | Fiber 0.4g | Sugar 13g | Protein 0.1g

Chocolate Frosting

Prep Time: 15 minutes.

Cook Time: 0 minutes.

Serves: 8

Ingredients:

- 2 cups confectioners' sugar, sifted
- 3 tablespoons of milk powder
- ½ cup unsweetened cocoa powder
- 6 tablespoons vegetable shortening

Preparation:

1. Beat shortening with sugar with cocoa powder and milk powder in a blender until creamy.

2. Refrigerate this frosting for 30 minutes.

3. Serve.

4. Mix with a spoon until smooth. Makes about 1/4 cup.

Serving Suggestion: Add the frosting to a piping bag and pipe it on top of plain cakes and muffins.

Variation Tip: Add cream cheese to the frosting to make it richer in taste.

Nutritional Information Per Serving:

Calories 135 | Fat 15g |Sodium 212mg | Carbs 19g | Fiber 0.4g | Sugar 9g | Protein 1.3g

Buttercream Frosting

Prep Time: 15 minutes.

Cook Time: 0 minutes.

Serves: 8

Ingredients:

- 2 cups icing sugar, sifted
- 3 tablespoons of milk powder
- 6 tablespoons butter

Preparation:

1. Beat butter with sugar and milk powder in a pastry blender.
2. Refrigerate this frosting for 30 minutes.
3. Serve.

Serving Suggestion: Add the frosting to a piping bag and pipe it on top of plain cakes and muffins.

Variation Tip: Add cream cheese to the frosting to make it richer in taste.

Nutritional Information Per Serving:

Calories 142 | Fat 14g |Sodium 224mg | Carbs 28g | Fiber 0.4g | Sugar 12g | Protein 2.3g

Pecan Frosting

Prep Time: 15 minutes.

Cook Time: 0 minutes.

Serves: 5 cups

Ingredients:

- 3 tablespoons butter
- 1/2 cup pecans
- 1 (14-oz.) can sweeten condensed milk

Preparation:

1. Blend pecans with butter and milk in a food processor until pureed.
2. Serve.

Serving Suggestion: Add the frosting to a piping bag and pipe it on top of plain cakes and muffins.

Variation Tip: Add cream cheese to the frosting to make it richer in taste.

Nutritional Information Per Serving:

Calories 135 | Fat 18g |Sodium 132mg | Carbs 14g | Fiber 1.1g | Sugar 5.9g | Protein 11g

Strawberry Frosting

Prep Time: 15 minutes.

Cook Time: 0 minutes.

Serves: 16

Ingredients:

- ½ pound fresh strawberries, sliced
- ½ cup butter softened
- 1 1/4 cups powdered sugar
- 1 teaspoon vanilla extract

Preparation:

1. Blend fresh strawberries in a food processor until pureed.
2. Beat butter with sugar and vanilla in a mixing bowl with a hand mixer until creamy.
3. Add strawberry puree and mix well.
4. Serve.

Serving Suggestion: Add the frosting to a piping bag and pipe it on top of plain cakes and muffins.

Variation Tip: Add cream cheese to the frosting to make it richer in taste.

Nutritional Information Per Serving:

Calories 107 | Fat 5g |Sodium 51mg | Carbs 14g | Fiber 12g | Sugar 13g | Protein 11g

Banana Frosting

Prep Time: 15 minutes.

Cook Time: 0 minutes.

Serves: 11

Ingredients:

- ¼ cup butter, softened
- ½ cup mashed bananas
- ½ teaspoon lemon juice
- ½ teaspoon vanilla extract
- 3 ¼ cups confectioners' sugar

Preparation:

1. Blend butter, bananas, lemon juice, vanilla extract and sugar in a food processor until pureed.
2. Serve.

Serving Suggestion: Add the frosting to a piping bag and pipe it on top of plain cakes and muffins.

Variation Tip: Add cream cheese to the frosting to make it richer in taste.

Nutritional Information Per Serving:

Calories 185 | Fat 4.35g |Sodium 532mg | Carbs 37g | Fiber 0.4g | Sugar 12g | Protein 0.3g

Chocolate Fudge Frosting

Prep Time: 15 minutes.

Cook Time: 0 minutes.

Serves: 12

Ingredients:

- ½ cup butter
- 3 (1 ounce) squares chocolate, melted
- 1-pound confectioners' sugar
- ½ teaspoon vanilla extract
- ¾ cup milk

Preparation:

1. Blend butter with sugar, milk and vanilla extract in a food processor until fluffy.
2. Add melted chocolate and mix well.
3. Serve.

Serving Suggestion: Add the frosting to a piping bag and pipe it on top of plain cakes and muffins.

Variation Tip: Add cream cheese to the frosting to make it richer in taste.

Nutritional Information Per Serving:

Calories 258 | Fat 11g |Sodium 62mg | Carbs 41g | Fiber 0.9g | Sugar 19g | Protein 1.5g

Blueberry Frosting

Prep Time: 15 minutes.

Cook Time: 0 minutes.

Serves: 16

Ingredients:

- 8 ounces fresh blueberries
- 1 cup butter
- 3 cups powdered sugar
- 1 teaspoon vanilla

Preparation:

1. Blend blueberries in a food processor until pureed.

2. Beat butter with sugar and vanilla in a mixing bowl with a hand mixer until creamy.

3. Add the blueberry puree and mix well.

4. Serve.

Serving Suggestion: Add the frosting to a piping bag and pipe it on top of plain cakes and muffins.

Variation Tip: Add cream cheese to the frosting to make it richer in taste.

Nutritional Information Per Serving:

Calories 198 | Fat 11g |Sodium 101mg | Carbs 24g | Fiber 1.3g | Sugar 12g | Protein 14.1g

Delicious Recipes

Cheese Balls

Prep Time: 15 minutes.

Cook Time: 15 minutes.

Serves: 6

Ingredients:

- 2 tablespoons margarine
- 1 tablespoon self-rising flour
- ¼ cup cheese, grated
- ¼ cup rice krispies

Preparation:

1. Mix margarine with flour, cheese and rice Krispies in a bowl.
2. Make small golf-ball sized balls out of this mixture.
3. Place these balls in the easy bake oven pan.
4. Bake them for 15 minutes in the easy bake oven.
5. Serve.

Serving Suggestion: Serve these balls with ketchup on the side.

Variation Tip: Add crumbled bacon to the batter before making balls.

Nutritional Information Per Serving:

Calories 317 | Fat 12g |Sodium 79mg | Carbs 14.8g | Fiber 1.1g | Sugar 8g | Protein 15g

Chocolate Balls

Prep Time: 15 minutes.

Cook Time: 0 minutes.

Serves: 8

Ingredients:

- 2 chocolate cookies
- 1 tablespoon coconut
- 1 tablespoon condensed milk, sweetened
- Sprinkles, chocolate

Preparation:

1. Crush cookies in a blender and mix them with cocoa and coconut.
2. Add condensed milk and mix well until it makes a dough.
3. Make 1-inch round balls out of this mixture and roll the balls in the sprinkles.
4. Serve.

Serving Suggestion: Serve the balls with white chocolate on top.

Variation Tip: Add chopped nuts to the prepared dough.

Nutritional Information Per Serving:

Calories 295 | Fat 3g |Sodium 355mg | Carbs 20g | Fiber 1g | Sugar 15g | Protein 1g

Bacon Roll-Ups

Prep Time: 15 minutes.

Cook Time: 15 minutes.

Serves: 6

Ingredients:

- 1/8 cup sour cream
- 1/8 teaspoon onion salt
- 1 tablespoon bacon bits
- ¼ 8oz. package crescent rolls

Preparation:

1. Separate the crescent rolls and spread them on the working surface. Cut each roll into four parts.
2. Mix bacon bits with onion salt and sour cream.
3. Spread this prepared mixture on top of each crescent roll piece.
4. Roll all the pieces and place them in the easy bake oven pan.
5. Bake all the rolls for 15 minutes.
6. Serve.

Serving Suggestion: Serve the roll-ups with tomato ketchup.

Variation Tip: Add cheese to the roll-ups.

Nutritional Information Per Serving:

Calories 153 | Fat 8.9g |Sodium 340mg | Carbs 24.7g | Fiber 1.2g | Sugar 11.3g | Protein 5.3g

Apple Tortilla

Prep Time: 15 minutes.

Cook Time: 25 minutes.

Serves: 4

Ingredients:

- 2 tablespoons apple pie filling
- 1 (8 inches) flour tortillas
- 1/8 teaspoon ground cinnamon

Preparation:

1. Cut the tortilla in size suitable to fit the easy bake oven pan.

2. Add apple pie filling at the center of the tortilla in a vertical line leaving 1-inch space from top and bottom.

3. Sprinkle cinnamon over the apple pie filling.

4. Fold the tortilla from top and bottom, then roll the tortilla to seal the filling inside.

5. Place this tortilla in the easy bake oven pan.

6. Bake this roll for 20 minutes in the easy bake oven.

7. Serve.

Serving Suggestion: Serve the tortilla with maple syrup.

Variation Tip: Use strawberry filling instead of apple filling.

Nutritional Information Per Serving:

Calories 117 | Fat 21g |Sodium 46mg | Carbs 32g | Fiber 1.8g | Sugar 12g | Protein 13.5g

Banana Pizza

Prep Time: 15 minutes.

Cook Time: 20 minutes.

Serves: 4

Ingredients:

- 1 sugar cookie dough
- 1 cup whipped cream
- 2 tablespoons sliced banana
- 2 tablespoons strawberries, sliced
- 2 tablespoons crushed pineapple, drained
- 2 tablespoons grapes, halved

Preparation:

1. Spread the cookie dough in a baking pan evenly.
2. Bake this dough for 20 minutes in the easy bake oven.
3. Allow the dough to cool over a wire rack and spread the whipped cream on top.
4. Add bananas, strawberries, pineapple, and grapes on top.
5. Serve.

Serving Suggestion: Serve the pizza with caramel sauce or chocolate syrup on top.

Variation Tip: Add walnuts to the toppings.

Nutritional Information Per Serving:

Calories 398 | Fat 14g |Sodium 272mg | Carbs 34g | Fiber 1g | Sugar 19.3g | Protein 1.3g

Dessert Pizza

Prep Time: 15 minutes.

Cook Time: 5 minutes.

Serves: 6

Ingredients:

Cookie Dough:

- 7 teaspoons shortening
- 7 teaspoons Sugar
- 1 pinch Salt
- 1/4 cup flour
- 1/8 teaspoon baking powder

- 1/8 teaspoon vanilla

Cream Cheese Topping:

- 1/4 cup cream cheese, room temp
- 1/4 cup Sugar

- 1/4 teaspoon vanilla

Topping:

- Fruit slices
- Banana
- Strawberries

- Apples
- Blueberries
- Mini chocolate chips

Preparation:

1. Beat butter with salt and sugar in a bowl until creamy.

2. Add vanilla, baking powder, and flour, then mix until it makes a smooth dough.

3. Sprinkle a teaspoon of flour on the working counter.

4. Roll the prepared dough on the floured surface and use a cookie cutter to cut 1-inch round circles.

5. Place these circles on a baking sheet and bake for 5 minutes in the easy bake oven.

6. Beat cream cheese with vanilla and sugar in a bowl until creamy.

7. Spread this cream cheese mixture on top of each baked cookie dough.

8. Garnish with fruits and chocolate chips.

9. Serve.

Serving Suggestion: Serve the pizza with caramel sauce or chocolate syrup on top.

Variation Tip: Add chopped nuts to the toppings.

Nutritional Information Per Serving:

Calories 271 | Fat 15g |Sodium 108mg | Carbs 33g | Fiber 1g | Sugar 26g | Protein 4g

Nachos

Prep Time: 15 minutes.

Cook Time: 9 minutes.

Serves: 2

Ingredients:

- 4 teaspoons cheese spread, soft
- 1 tablespoon Salsa
- 1 cup nacho chips

Preparation:

1. Preheat your easy bake oven for 15 minutes.
2. Meanwhile, mix cheese with salsa in a bowl.
3. Spread the prepared mixture in a baking pan and bake for 9 minutes in the easy bake oven.
4. Serve.

Serving Suggestion: Serve the nachos with guacamole on top.

Variation Tip: Add crumbled bacon as a topping.

Nutritional Information Per Serving:

Calories 245 | Fat 14g |Sodium 122mg | Carbs 23.3g | Fiber 1.2g | Sugar 12g | Protein 4.3g

Conclusion

Hey, kids! I hope you enjoyed baking those lovely treats! If you haven't, then gone ahead, put on your aprons, and let's get started!

This cookbook provides you all the easy bake oven recipes that will help you cook and bake a variety of treats without having to ask about the recipes from grown-ups! This is the time to explore your inner baker and bake like professionals with your easy bake oven. I know it is super challenging to take exact proportions of the ingredients and then mix them together in different styles to bake different treats, but the recipes in this cookbook will ease down the process for you! There are no complicated preparation steps, and none of the ingredients are challenging to find! Every supermarket offers you those cake mixes, some sprinkles, mixers, fruits, and chocolates, and that's what you must have found in this cookbook.

So, stop waiting around to ask somebody how to bake your first cake or cookies, simply pick your favorite recipes from this cookbook and give it a try. Learning is a hit and trial process; you can't expect great results on your first try! It always takes time to master your baking skills, be patient, and start with the baby steps. One day you are going to be an excellent baker or chef; you just don't know that yet!

And here is yet another reminder for all the parents out there! As you keep an eye on your kids while they bake in their easy bake oven, do not overindulge in the process; give your children complete freedom to learn on their own! These early life experiences are important for every kid to learn some basic life skills like management, organizing, and cleaning. Guide your kids about everything, then step back and let them do that in their own way. You will be amazed by their creativity and by the power of their imagination.

Have happy baking!

Lightning Source UK Ltd.
Milton Keynes UK
UKHW051906101122
411897UK00003B/61